Table of Contents

Elizabeth Cady Stanton   *Lucy Stone*   *Carrie Chapman Catt*   *Alice Paul*

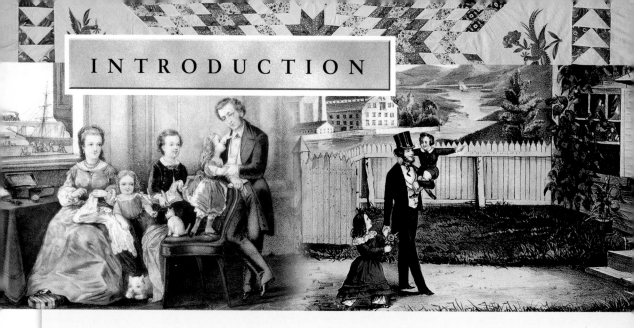

America in 1840

A WOMAN'S PLACE

*T*he struggle by American women to win the right to vote really starts in the 1840s. At that time, most people believed that a woman's natural place was in the home. Her job was to care for her husband and family. This was called "**true womanhood.**"

This view about women's role affected every part of their lives. Women's legal rights were limited.

We're speaking here of free women. Slave women had very few rights. But even free women could not vote, sit on juries, or hold public office. People of the time felt that women were too emotional to work in business or take part in politics. By law in most states, a married woman's property belonged to her husband. If she had a job, her wages belonged to her husband. And if a couple divorced, their children belonged to the husband.

ANN ROSSI

CREATED EQUAL

WOMEN CAMPAIGN FOR THE RIGHT TO VOTE
1840–1920

NATIONAL GEOGRAPHIC

Washington, D.C.

PICTURE CREDITS: Cover Bettmann/CORBIS; pp. 1 (right), 3 (bottom right), 11, 13 (bottom), 14, 18 (top), 20, 25 (middle, right, bottom), 29 (right), 32 (top), 33 (top), 35 (top right), 37 (bottom), 40 CORBIS; pp. 2, 7, 10, 12, 16 (right), 17 (left & right), 18, 24, 25 (top), 32 (bottom), 34, 36, 38 Bettmann/CORBIS; p. 3 (3rd from bottom left) State Historical Society of Wisconsin Visual Archives; pp. 1 (left), 3 (bottom left), 8 National Portrait Gallery, Smithsonian Institution/Art Resource, NY; pp. 2–7 (border), 13–15 (border), 18–19 (border), 35–40 (border) Newark Museum/Art Resource, NY; pp. 3 (2nd from bottom left), 4 (left & right), 5 (bottom), 6, 9 (right), 16 (left), 22, 27 (bottom), 28, 32–33 (bkgd.), 33 (top) Library of Congress; p. 4 (left) Museum of the City of New York/CORBIS; p. 5 (left & right) Cynthia Hart Designer/CORBIS; pp. 9–11 (border), 21–27 (border) Jacqui Hurst/CORBIS; p. 13 (top right) Illustrated News; p. 18 (bkgd.) The Univ. of Rochester Library; p. 19 Hulton-Deutsch Collection/CORBIS; p. 21 (top right) Taxi/Getty Images; p. 23 Rykoff Collection/CORBIS; pp. 27 (top), 31 (top) National Women's Party, Sewall-Belmont House; pp. 29–31 (border) Buddy Mays/CORBIS; p. 31 (bottom) Life Magazine; p. 35 (bottom) David J. and Janice L. Frent Collection/CORBIS; p. 37 (top) AP/Wide World.

Library of Congress Cataloging-in-Publication Data

Rossi, Ann.
   Created equal : women campaign for the right to vote, 1840-1920 / by Ann Rossi.
     p. cm. — (Crossroads America)
     ISBN: 0-7922-8275-2
   Includes index.
   Summary: A brief history of American women's fight for voting rights.
   1. Women—Suffrage—United States—History—19th century—Juvenile literature.
2. Suffragists—United States—History—19th century—Juvenile literature. 3. Women's rights—United States—History—19th century—Juvenile literature. 4. Women—Suffrage—United States—History—20th century—Juvenile literature. 5. Suffragists—United States—History—20th century—Juvenile literature. 6. Women's rights—United States—History—20th century—Juvenile literature. [1. Women—Suffrage. 2. Women's rights—History.] I. Title. II. Series.
   JK1898.R67 2003
   324.6'23'0973—dc22
                                              2003019827

Produced through the worldwide resources of the National Geographic Society, John M. Fahey, Jr., President and Chief Executive Officer; Gilbert M. Grosvenor, Chairman of the Board; Nina D. Hoffman, Executive Vice President and President, Books and Education Publishing; Ericka Markman, President, Children's Books and Education Publishing Group; Nancy Feresten, Vice President, Children's Books, Editor-in-Chief; Steve Mico, Vice President Education Publishing Group, Editorial Director; Marianne Hiland, Editorial Manager; Anita Schwartz, Project Editor; Tara Peterson, Editorial Assistant; Jim Hiscott, Design Manager; Linda McKnight, Art Director; Diana Bourdrez, Anne Whittle, Photo Research; Matt Wascavage, Manager of Publishing Services; Sean Philpotts, Production Coordinator; Jane Ponton, Production Artist; Susan Donnelly, Children's Books Project Editor. Production: Clifton M. Brown III, Manufacturing and Quality Control.

PROGRAM DEVELOPMENT
Gare Thompson Associates, Inc.

CONSULTANTS/REVIEWERS
Dr. Margit E. McGuire, School of Education, Seattle University, Seattle, Washington

BOOK DESIGN
Steven Curtis Design, Inc.

NATIONAL GEOGRAPHIC SOCIETY
1145 17th Street, N.W.
Washington, D.C. 20036-4688

Printed in Mexico

At this time, very few men went to college. But almost no women at all did. Many people believed that women only needed to learn things that would help them be good wives and mothers. Few women received more than a grade school education. In 1833, only one college in the United States—Oberlin College—admitted women.

WOMAN'S "SPHERE"

A WOMAN WONDERS WHAT THE WORLD IS LIKE OUTSIDE HER "SPHERE"—OR NATURAL PLACE.

WHY WOMEN WANTED REFORM

During the early 1800s, many Americans worked to improve social conditions. Religious groups helped spur this reform effort. And because women played a large role in church life, they also became involved in reform. One of the major reform efforts of this time was the **temperance movement.**

This was the fight to stop the sale and use of alcoholic beverages. Heavy drinking was a very serious problem in America in the early 1800s. Women and their children were among the chief victims of male drunkenness. So, many women worked for the temperance movement.

WOMEN IN THE TEMPERANCE MOVEMENT SING HYMNS IN FRONT OF A SALOON.

Slavery also concerned many Americans. Some joined the **abolitionist movement.** They worked for the abolition, or end, of slavery. But women in the abolitionist movement came to realize something important. In some ways, their situation was like that of slaves.

Many women in the temperance and abolitionist movements came to believe that they had to fight for their own rights as women. And if they wanted to do this, women first needed the right to vote, or **suffrage.**

These women reformers, called suffragists, believed that voting was the key to change.

IN THEIR OWN WORDS

❝Make the whole world homelike.❞

Frances E. Willard, temperance movement leader

WOMEN ATTEND AN ABOLITIONIST MEETING IN BOSTON IN 1851.

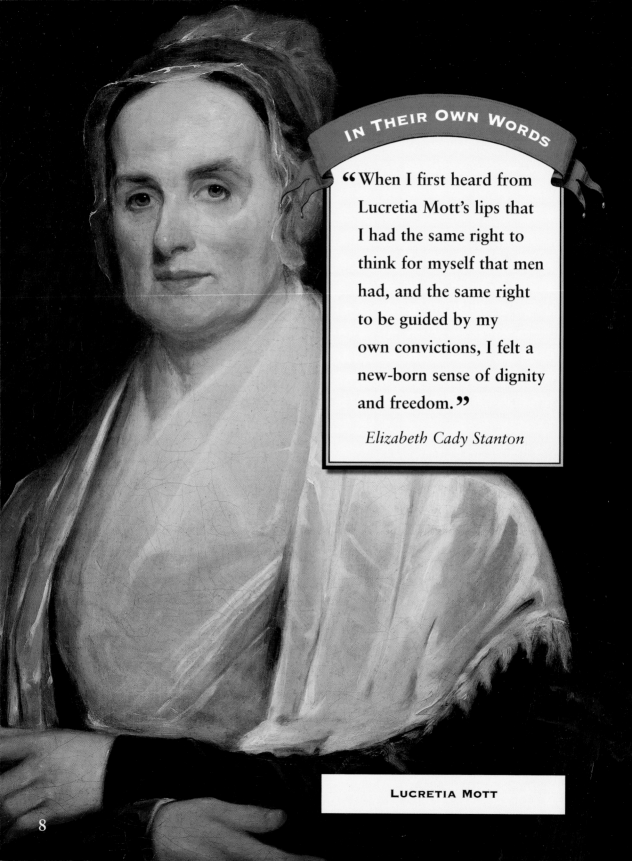

"When I first heard from Lucretia Mott's lips that I had the same right to think for myself that men had, and the same right to be guided by my own convictions, I felt a new-born sense of dignity and freedom."

Elizabeth Cady Stanton

LUCRETIA MOTT

Reaching for the Vote

KINDLING THE FLAME

Many male reformers did not think women should work alongside them. So some women formed their own groups. Lucretia Mott was one of them. She was born in 1793 to a **Quaker** family. Quakers believed that all people—men and women, black and white—were equal. Mott started a women's anti-slavery society in Philadelphia.

In 1840, Mott went to London to attend the first World's Anti-Slavery Convention. Many men did not want women to take part. After much arguing, women were allowed to attend. But they had to sit behind a curtain to be neither seen nor heard. Without knowing it, the men had kindled the American woman suffrage movement.

Mott was angered by the way women were treated at the Convention. Another woman who was outraged was Elizabeth Cady Stanton. She was attending the convention with her husband.

Stanton was born into a well-to-do family in 1815. When her brother died at 21, young Elizabeth remembered her father saying, "Oh, my daughter, I wish you were a boy!"

Stanton's experience at the World's Anti-Slavery Convention changed her. She and Mott became close friends. The two women discussed how wrong it was to ban women from taking part in the convention. They decided to try to change the way women were treated. They agreed to hold a women's rights convention in the United States.

THE CONVENTION AT SENECA FALLS

Eight years later, in 1848, Lucretia Mott, Elizabeth Cady Stanton, and three other women organized a women's rights convention in Seneca Falls, New York. They wrote a document that listed their beliefs about women's rights. It was called the "Declaration of Sentiments." Stanton modeled it after the Declaration of Independence.

One **resolution** caused heated debate. It called for women to have the right to vote. It was the first time in the United States that women had publicly demanded the right to vote. In the end, 68 women and 32 men signed the Declaration. The woman suffrage movement had begun.

Most newspapers reporting on the convention made fun of the women. But Stanton felt any publicity got people to think about women's rights. She was correct. In time, women's rights conventions were held throughout the nation. A woman's right to vote became a key issue.

ELIZABETH CADY STANTON SPEAKING AT SENECA FALLS

IN THEIR OWN WORDS

"We hold these truths to be self-evident: that all men and women are created equal."

Elizabeth Cady Stanton

A NEW PARTNERSHIP

Elizabeth Cady Stanton had lots of ideas about women's rights that she wanted to share with others. She was an excellent writer. But family life left her little time. In addition, Stanton's father, and at times her husband, had been shocked and embarrassed by her occasional public appearances. Her father even threatened to write her out of his will if she continued to speak in public. Stanton needed someone to deliver her speeches.

She found her in Susan B. Anthony. Anthony was born in 1820. She came from a large Quaker family. When she was 17, Anthony started teaching to help her family. She also joined a temperance group. Soon she was organizing events and training other women. One day, Anthony tried to speak at a temperance convention. She was furious when the chairman told her that women were not invited to speak. They were "to listen and learn." At about this time, Anthony met Elizabeth Cady Stanton. Stanton quickly convinced Anthony to join her in the fight for women's rights.

Anthony was very valuable. She was unmarried, tireless, and a good organizer. She also had a strong, clear voice. She had the time to travel and gather public support for the women's movement. She raised funds, started petition campaigns, and gave public speeches. She also researched laws and collected facts for Stanton. Their partnership lasted more than 50 years.

SUSAN B. ANTHONY AND ELIZABETH CADY STANTON

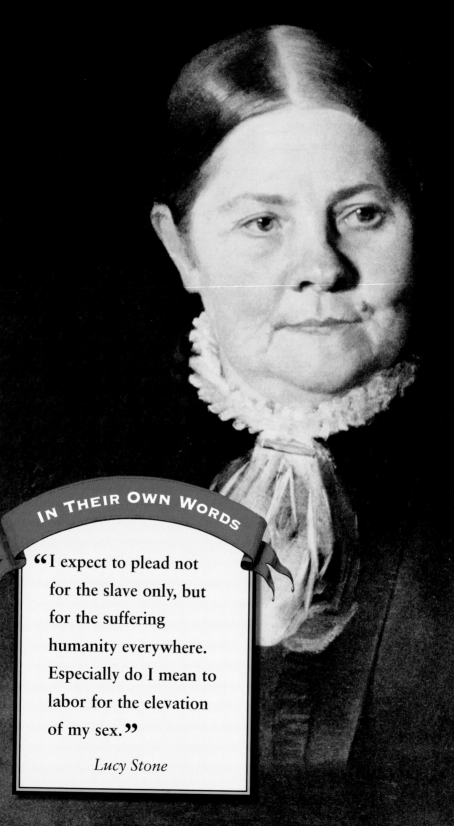

"I expect to plead not for the slave only, but for the suffering humanity everywhere. Especially do I mean to labor for the elevation of my sex."

Lucy Stone

CHAPTER 2

The Struggle Continues

LUCY STONE

**STONE GIVING
A SPEECH**

*L*ucy Stone was born on a farm in Massachusetts in 1818. She was one of nine children. When Stone was born, her mother said, "I am sorry it is a girl. A woman's life is so hard."

Stone worked hard at home. She worked hard at school too. Stone desperately wanted to go to college. But her family did not think college was for women. She was very determined. Stone started teaching when she was 16. She saved her money. Nine years later, Stone went to Oberlin College.

Stone was asked to write a speech for graduation. She learned that a man would make the speech because women were not allowed to speak in public. She refused to write the speech.

Stone wanted to help people who were unfairly treated. She became an abolitionist and supporter of women's rights.

Stone was a wonderful speaker. When she married Henry Blackwell in 1855, her opponents hoped she would stop speaking in public. One wrote a poem praising the man who would "with a wedding kiss" shut "the mouth of Lucy Stone."

But Henry Blackwell was a supporter of women's rights. The couple saw themselves as equal partners in marriage. They wrote their own wedding vows—and Lucy Stone kept her own name.

IN THE 1850S, SOME REFORMERS ALSO WANTED TO CHANGE HOW WOMEN DRESSED. "BLOOMERS" WERE LOOSE-FITTING TROUSERS.

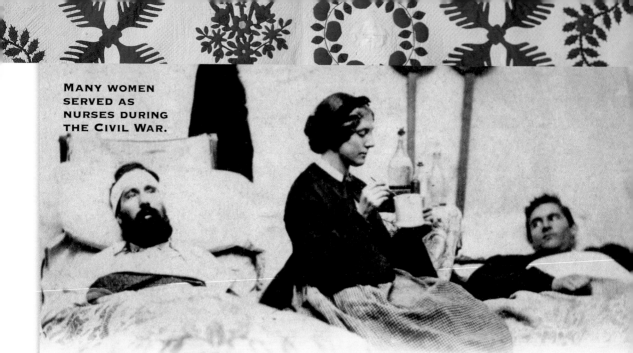

MANY WOMEN SERVED AS NURSES DURING THE CIVIL WAR.

WAR BRINGS NEW DUTIES

The Civil War began in 1861. The need to deal with wartime problems halted the women's rights movement for a time. On both sides, many women helped with the war effort. Some nursed wounded soldiers. Others raised money to buy medical supplies. Many women supported their families while their husbands and sons fought in the war. They ran plantations, farms, and businesses. They worked in factories and in government offices.

Meanwhile, Elizabeth Cady Stanton and Susan B. Anthony founded the National Women's Loyal League.

Their goal was to help the Union war effort, end slavery—and support women's rights.

The League collected nearly 400,000 signatures to convince Congress to outlaw slavery. In December 1865, eight months after the Civil War ended, the Constitution's **Thirteenth Amendment** outlawed slavery.

Women had gained leadership skills from their wartime experiences. After the war, some women used these skills to start social agencies. Clara Barton, for example, founded the American Red Cross. Some women also used their skills for the cause of women's rights.

CONFLICTS DEVELOP IN THE MOVEMENT

A year after the Civil War ended, Stanton, Anthony, and others formed the American Equal Rights Association to fight for the voting rights of women and African Americans. The **Fourteenth Amendment** had just been proposed. It gave former slaves citizenship and some protection of their civil rights, including the right to vote. But this last right only applied to males over 21. Stanton and Anthony wanted the word *male* removed from the amendment.

Some people thought that adding woman suffrage to the amendment was not a good idea. They feared that lawmakers would not vote for it. They felt women should wait to get the vote. The amendment—with the word *male* still in—became law in 1868.

Two years later, the **Fifteenth Amendment** was proposed. It strengthened the Fourteenth Amendment's protection of African-American voting rights.

The Fifteenth Amendment stated that the right of citizens to vote could not be denied because of race, color, or whether they had been slaves. If the Fifteenth Amendment could only be broadened to include women! Here was an opportunity! But again, some who wanted to protect African-American voting rights thought that the women's issue made their fight more difficult. Women should wait. But some thought women should not have to wait.

IN THEIR OWN WORDS

"I will cut off this right arm of mine before I will ever work for or demand the ballot for the Negro and not the woman."

Susan B. Anthony

15

Should Women Wait to Vote?

Susan B. Anthony first met Lucy Stone at a women's rights convention in 1852. They were good friends until they strongly disagreed over the Fifteenth Amendment. They had opposite points of view on whether women should wait for the vote.

Stone thought women should wait. She supported the Fifteenth Amendment because she thought it was important to get voting rights for African-American men first. Then people could try to win voting rights for women.

We are lost if we turn away and argue for one class. Woman has an ocean of wrongs and the negro too has an ocean of wrongs. There are two great oceans; in the one is the black man, and in the other is the woman. But I hope that the Fifteenth Amendment will be adopted in every State. I will be thankful in my soul if anybody can get out of the terrible pit.

AFRICAN AMERICANS VOTING FOR THE FIRST TIME

Anthony did not want women to wait for the vote. She opposed the Fifteenth Amendment because it did not give voting rights to both men and women.

The Fifteenth Amendment would not mean equal rights. It would put two million colored men in the position of tyrants over two million colored women, who until now had at least been the equals of the men at their side. If you will not give the whole loaf of justice to the entire people, if you are determined to extend the suffrage piece by piece, then give it first to women.

WOMEN ATTEMPTING TO VOTE IN 1871

The Fifteenth Amendment became law in 1870. The conflict over the amendment ended the friendship of Lucy Stone and Susan B. Anthony. It also split the women's rights movement for many years.

17

THE MOVEMENT SPLITS AND UNITES

Susan B. Anthony and Elizabeth Cady Stanton continued to work hard for votes for women. They ran a newspaper called *The Revolution*. The women printed articles that supported issues such as easy-to-get divorces. Stanton called men "tyrants" and used other anti-male language. Such things shocked many people in the late 1800s.

Moderates thought the woman suffrage movement would lose support as a result of the **radical** articles published in *The Revolution*. Finally, in 1869, the suffragists split into two competing organizations.

JOIN THE NATIONAL WOMAN'S SUFFRAGE ASSOCIATION

JOIN THE NATIONAL WOMENS SUFFRAGE ASSOCIATION

A MEETING OF THE NATIONAL WOMAN SUFFRAGE ASSOCIATION

Stanton and Anthony formed the National Woman Suffrage Association (NWSA). It did not allow men to be members. NWSA worked for a Constitutional amendment to give women the right to vote in national elections.

Lucy Stone and others formed the American Woman Suffrage Association (AWSA). It focused on winning woman suffrage state by state. AWSA allowed men to become members.

Neither group reached its goals. In 1878, NWSA persuaded a California senator to introduce a Constitutional amendment for woman suffrage. Congress did not pass it. But the amendment became known as the "Susan B. Anthony Amendment." It was brought up at each session of Congress for the next 42 years.

Finally, more than 20 years after they split, the groups joined together. They formed the National American Woman Suffrage Association (NAWSA) in 1890. Stanton was its president for two years. Susan B. Anthony followed her. Anthony stepped down in 1900. It was time for younger women to take over.

" Principle, not policy; Justice, not favors. Men, their rights and nothing more; Women, their rights, and nothing less. "

Susan B. Anthony, motto of The Revolution

SUFFRAGISTS ON A STREET CORNER AROUND 1905

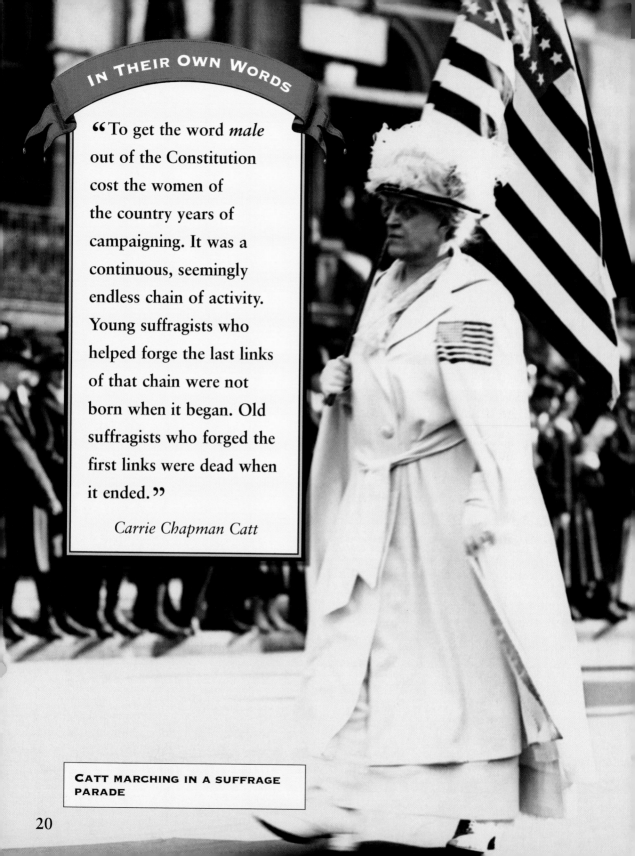

"To get the word *male* out of the Constitution cost the women of the country years of campaigning. It was a continuous, seemingly endless chain of activity. Young suffragists who helped forge the last links of that chain were not born when it began. Old suffragists who forged the first links were dead when it ended."

Carrie Chapman Catt

CATT MARCHING IN A SUFFRAGE PARADE

CHAPTER 3

Behind the Barricades

A NEW LEADER FOR A NEW CENTURY

TWO GIRLS IN A SUFFRAGE MARCH

*M*any changes had taken place in the late 1800s. More women went to college. Many more women were working outside the home. In some states, married women could own property and keep their wages. But by 1900, only four states had given women the right to vote. Carrie Chapman Catt was largely responsible for the success in Colorado. She had superb organizational and fundraising skills. She was also a forceful speaker.

Catt was born in 1859 in Wisconsin. As a girl, she asked why her mother didn't vote in the presidential elections, like her father did. Carrie was told that voting was too important to leave to women.

She thought that was unfair and decided right then to do something about it someday.

Catt worked her way through college. After college, she first became a teacher and then a school official. She also began working for woman suffrage. Susan B. Anthony recommended Catt as the next president of the National American Woman Suffrage Association. Catt was the president from 1900 to 1904 and again from 1915 to 1920. She doubled its membership to two million. She continued NAWSA's efforts to win woman suffrage in individual states.

THE ANTI-SUFFRAGISTS

Men and women who did not think that women should get the vote were known as **anti-suffragists**. They were called "antis" for short.

Antis wanted things to stay the same. They feared many changes would occur if women won the vote. Antis thought women would no longer let men make decisions. They believed that families would be destroyed.

Anti-suffragists argued that women already had too much to do. Voting would be another burden. Antis also pointed out that women's lives had not improved in states with woman suffrage. For example, women's wages had not increased.

As support for woman suffrage increased, female antis organized. They tried to persuade politicians and citizens that woman suffrage was wrong. By 1916, the National Association Opposed to Woman Suffrage had branches in 25 states.

OFFICE OF AN ANTI-SUFFRAGE ORGANIZATION

Certain industries also opposed woman suffrage. Some of them gave money to the antis. They feared that women who had political power would be able to press for better wages. These industries tried to keep secret their help to the antis. Many of them, such as cloth manufacturers, employed huge numbers of women.

Liquor manufacturers were also against woman suffrage. They feared that women would use their political power to stop the sale and drinking of alcohol. Many women supported the temperance movement.

Many white Southerners also opposed woman suffrage. Some white Southern men feared they would lose political power if black women won the vote. They thought that black women would be more likely to vote than white women. They believed that white Southern women were too modest to vote.

ANTI-SUFFRAGE POSTCARD SHOWING A WOMAN RULING HER HUSBAND

IN THEIR OWN WORDS

❝ The vote is part of man's work. Ballot-box, cartridge box, jury box, sentry box all go together in his part of life. Woman cannot step in and take the responsibilities and duties of voting without assuming his place very largely. ❞

Emily Bissell,
anti-suffrage leader

ALICE PAUL

Elizabeth Cady Stanton had predicted that the new generation of suffragists would not wait patiently for the vote. She was right. Some women organized marches to draw attention to woman suffrage. Others formed new organizations.

In 1913, Alice Paul founded what became the National Woman's Party. Like Lucretia Mott and Susan B. Anthony, Paul was a Quaker. She grew up thinking men and women were equals. Paul brought new energy to the woman suffrage movement. In 1913, she organized thousands of marchers for a woman suffrage parade in Washington, D.C. Later, Paul and a group of women met with U.S. President Woodrow Wilson. They asked for his help in passing the Anthony Amendment. Wilson replied that individual states should give women the vote, not Congress.

In January 1917, Paul organized groups of women to **picket,** or carry protest signs, in front of the White House six days a week. The signs demanded woman suffrage.

Paul and other women were arrested during their protests. One time, Paul went on a hunger strike in prison. Guards forced her to eat. The event made headline news. Due to public pressure, the women were released from prison. But the picketing did not stop until Wilson changed his position on woman suffrage.

ALICE PAUL GOT SEVEN MONTHS BECAUSE SHE OPPOSED A POLITICAL PARTY **WE DEMAND** THAT SHE BE TREATED AS A POLITICAL OFFENDER

SUFFRAGISTS PROTESTING IMPRISONMENT OF ALICE PAUL

MR. PRESIDENT HOW LONG MUST WOMEN WAIT FOR LIBERTY?

MEMBERS OF
NATIONAL
WOMAN'S
PARTY
PICKETING

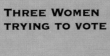

PRESIDENT WILSON SAYS
the time to support Woman Suffr

WOMAN
SUFFRAGE
PARADE

THREE WOMEN
TRYING TO VOTE

ALICE
PAUL

25

EDNA PURTELL

In 1918, Edna Purtell was a teenager working as a filing clerk in Connecticut. She took a week's vacation to go to Washington, D.C. But Purtell was not going sightseeing. She was a suffragist. Purtell and hundreds of other suffragists were marching in a parade. They were angry that the Senate had gone on vacation without voting on the woman suffrage amendment.

The protesters carried banners and shouted slogans as they marched to the White House. They wanted President Wilson to speak with them. Instead, the police arrested the protesters. A policeman tried to pull a banner out of Purtell's hands. He broke two of her fingers.

Purtell and other protesters were taken to a building that was in such bad shape that it had been declared "unfit for human habitation." The protesters went on a hunger strike. Many of them became ill.

Senators and citizens alike were shocked by conditions at the place where the protesters were being held. They demanded that the protesters be released. As soon as they were, the women applied for a permit to hold another protest.

IN THEIR OWN WORDS

" When I came back, my boss said, 'You know, Miss Purtell, you're liked very well here, but we don't want you to be talking about suffrage.' I said to him, 'Mr. Batterson, during work hours I'll take care of my job. But once I get in that elevator, I'll talk about anything I want.' "

Edna Purtell

"JAILED FOR FREEDOM" PIN GIVEN TO IMPRISONED SUFFRAGISTS

SUFFRAGIST PARADE IN WASHINGTON, D.C.

ALICE PAUL TOASTING
RATIFICATION OF THE
NINETEENTH AMENDMENT
(WITH GRAPE JUICE)

Passing the Nineteenth Amendment

WOMEN IN NEW YORK CITY VOTING IN THEIR FIRST ELECTION IN 1920

AN ORGANIZED EFFORT

On June 4, 1919, American women moved a giant step closer to winning the vote. The Senate voted in favor of the proposed **Nineteenth Amendment**, giving women the right to vote. Now the fight to ratify, or approve, the amendment would go to the individual states. Lawmakers in each state would vote on it. For the amendment to become law, three-quarters of the states would have to ratify it. In 1919, there were 48 states. That meant that 36 states had to ratify the amendment.

Carrie Chapman Catt, Alice Paul, and other suffragists knew that it was too soon to celebrate. Hard work lay ahead. They had to convince lawmakers in 36 states to support the amendment. The anti-suffragists, on the other hand, had to convince only 13 states to vote against suffrage.

Catt wasted no time. She sent messages to suffrage groups throughout the country. She urged them to meet with governors and other politicians in their states. Their job was to convince politicians to support suffrage.

Early on, Catt and her workers had figured out which states were most likely to vote for suffrage. Catt knew that woman suffrage would be least likely to win in the Southern states and the two New England states with anti-suffrage governors, Vermont and Connecticut. But she refused to ignore these states. She thought that any one of them might be the key to victory. She was right.

29

COUNTDOWN IN TENNESSEE

In March 1920, Washington became the 35th state to ratify the Nineteenth Amendment. Tennessee could be the deciding state. Suffragists traveled across Tennessee making speeches from a train called the "Tennessee Suffrage Special." Anti-suffragists and suffragists were doing everything they could to pressure lawmakers to support their cause.

The governor called a special session in August to vote on the amendment. The fight for ratification became known as the "War of the Roses." Lawmakers in favor of suffrage wore a yellow rose in their lapels. Antis wore a red rose. Even so, it was difficult to know whose side anyone was really on. One man wore a red-and-yellow rose! Lawmakers often changed their minds but not their roses.

Finally, it was time for the vote. It was very close. Only one more vote was needed. Suddenly, all eyes and ears were on Harry Burn, the youngest lawmaker. He wore a red rose. The suffragists' hearts sank.

But when Burn spoke, he voted for the amendment. Cheers burst from the suffragists. At long last, women in the United States could vote.

Burn had agonized over how he should vote. Many of his **constituents**, the people he represented, opposed woman suffrage. Others, including his mother, supported it. Finally, Burn voted the way his conscience and his mother wanted him to.

"CONGRATULATIONS" TO SUFFRAGISTS FROM HARRY BURN (FOREGROUND OF PHOTO) AND LADY LIBERTY (ON MAGAZINE COVER)

October 28, 1920   Vol. 76.   Copyright, 1920, Life Publishing Company   No. 1983   **Life**   Price 15 Cents

"Congratulations"

Political Cartoons

Newspapers often made fun of women who were seeking the right to vote. Many newspapers used cartoons to make their points.

SUFFRAGE LEADERS ATTACKING UNCLE SAM

SUSAN B. ANTHONY DRESSED AS UNCLE SAM

A NEW WOMAN VOTER LEAVING CHILDCARE TO HER HUSBAND

AN ANTI-SUFFRAGE CARTOON PRESENTING SUFFRAGISTS AS IDLE TROUBLEMAKERS

CARRIE CHAPMAN
CATT VOTING IN HER
FIRST ELECTION

34

CHAPTER 5

A YOUNG WOMAN AND A
JAZZ BAND HAVING FUN
AT THE BEACH IN 1922

Women Vote!

IMMEDIATE EFFECTS

In 1920, American women were able to vote in a national election for the first time. The suffragists urged all women to vote. They had worked hard to win this right. They also encouraged women to become active in politics.

But large numbers of women didn't rush to the voting booths. The percentage of women voting would not equal men for 30 years. Nor did women use their votes to push for social change.

A POLITICAL RIBBON FROM 1920 SHOWING THE SUPPORT OF A NEW WOMAN VOTER FOR REPUBLICAN PRESIDENTIAL CANDIDATE WARREN G. HARDING

Following World War I, many Americans wanted to forget about politics. They wanted to enjoy life. Many young women rebelled against the styles of their mothers. They did not want long dresses and long hair. Instead, young women cut their hair and wore short skirts. They danced and had fun.

But some suffragists stayed active. They wanted to help women in new ways. Carrie Chapman Catt thought that women needed information about political issues and candidates. As a result, the League of Women Voters was formed. Today, the League is a **nonpartisan** educational organization for women and men. It does not endorse, or support, candidates or political parties. The League encourages citizens to vote. It studies public issues, provides information, and makes recommendations.

JEANNETTE RANKIN OF MONTANA, FIRST WOMAN TO SERVE IN CONGRESS, BEING PRESENTED WITH THE FLAG THAT FLEW DURING THE VOTE ON THE NINETEENTH AMENDMENT

WOMEN IN PUBLIC LIFE

Many male politicians were relieved that women did not run for office as soon as they were able to vote. Yet soon, more and more women began running for local, state, and federal offices. Today women in the United States are mayors, lawmakers, and governors.

After women won the right to vote in 1920, other laws were passed that gave women equal rights with men. Over time, women used their political power to make many changes. In 1963, the Equal Pay Act required that men and women get the same pay for doing the same work. Today, federally funded schools and colleges must give men and women equal opportunities to attend classes and sports programs. Women and men have the same opportunities to borrow money from banks. They have the same job opportunities too. Today, many women work in jobs that were once for men only.

(LEFT TO RIGHT) GLORIA STEINEM, BELLA ABZUG, SHIRLEY CHISHOLM, AND BETTY FRIEDAN—WOMEN'S RIGHTS MOVEMENT LEADERS OF THE 1960S AND 1970S

SANDRA DAY O'CONNOR, FIRST WOMAN JUSTICE OF THE SUPREME COURT

Legacy

At Seneca Falls in 1848, Elizabeth Cady Stanton was the first American woman to publicly demand the right to vote. Her demand became a reality when the Nineteenth Amendment was passed. Only one woman who signed the Declaration of Sentiments lived to see the passage of the Nineteenth Amendment. Her name was Charlotte Woodward. She was 19 when she signed the resolution and in her 90s when the Nineteenth Amendment became law.

By 1920, women had won many other rights that women in 1848 did not have. They could own property, keep their wages, and sit on a jury. Women could get a good education and go to college. They had learned how to organize to push for changes to laws. Today, women are an important voting block. Politicians seek their votes. Political candidates cannot ignore issues that matter to women. Women are no longer without a voice in public affairs.

Glossary

ABOLITIONIST MOVEMENT
a reform movement that worked for the end of slavery

ANTI-SUFFRAGIST a person opposed to giving women the right to vote

CONSTITUENT one of a group of voters who elect a public official

FIFTEENTH AMENDMENT
change to the U.S. Constitution passed in 1870 to protect African-American voting rights

FOURTEENTH AMENDMENT
change to the U.S. Constitution passed in 1868 to make former slaves citizens

MODERATE a person opposed to extreme political views

NINETEENTH AMENDMENT
change to the U.S. Constitution passed in 1920 to give women the right to vote

NONPARTISAN not supporting a political party

PICKET carry protest signs

QUAKER belonging to the Society of Friends, a Christian religious group

RADICAL in favor of extreme political changes

RESOLUTION a formal statement of an opinion debated by an assembly

SUFFRAGE the right to vote

TEMPERANCE MOVEMENT
a reform movement that worked to stop the sale and use of alcoholic beverages

THIRTEENTH AMENDMENT
change to the U.S. Constitution passed in 1865 that outlawed slavery

"TRUE WOMANHOOD" belief common in America in the 1800s that married women should limit themselves to housework and childcare

Index